Self Knowledge for Beginners

Meditations, Rituals, Dream Journeys and more ...

Contact: www.HarryEilenstein.de
Harry.Eilenstein@web.de
Harry Eilenstein at youtube

Production and publishing house: BoD – Books on Demand, Norderstedt

ISBN: 9783753491165

Nothing is closer to oneself than one's own center –
but this center often is not very well known to oneself ...

Table of Contents

Preface

Writing a book about self-discovery is a delicate matter – simply because people are very different and see themselves and the world very differently.

From the point of view of almost all people, almost all other people are a bit strange – or even a bit more …

When you sit together with a person and talk, meditate together or perform rituals together, you can see who the other person might be. Then you can make somewhat more specific suggestions about self-discovery.

In a book, you can really only describe all the ways you have found yourself. But even then, what one can describe in terms of possibilities is still subjective – after all, these possibilities are only those that one has already found oneself, tried out and found useful.

Thus, while one can find a lot of suggestions in this book, one cannot find a universal recipe for finding one's own center.

After all, the need to recognize one's own center and to live one's own life is quite widespread – almost everyone wants to be the captain on one's own ship sailing on the sea of life.

This includes not only the light of self-knowledge but also the fire of courage, the air of clarity, the water of love and the earth of thriving. Therefore, each chapter of this book is divided into the four elements and the quintessence – in the hope that in this way as many people as possible will find something useful in this book.

The five chapters of this book are a gradual increase in the intensity of taking steps on the path to oneself. They also correspond roughly to the five-part "Exercise of the Middle Pillar" that is the central part of the "Kabbalistic Tree of Life". These five chapters are "resolution – contact – becoming familiar – deepening – radiance".

Of course, this does not at all mean that you have to do all the suggested contemplations, meditations, rituals, dream journeys, etc. in this order – you should always have a look what appeals to you and what you are curious about.

Even if other people can report about their experiences and make suggestions to others, everybody has to find his own way …

I Resolution

Every action begins with a decision – as long as it is not a pure reflex. But every decision has a prehistory from which it arises.

This is also true for the search for oneself.

I 1. Light: The Occasion

An action is meant to change something. So actions arise in situations where either something hurts or where something beckons. Unfortunately, in most cases the fear of pain is the motivation and not the hope of pleasure.

This could be more creative – and rediscovering one's center is a great help in orienting one's life again more to going towards the light than to running away from the shadows.

The feeling that something is not right or that in one area the possibilities are not yet exhausted is the beginning of the action. In order to come to the decision to go in search of oneself, there must be a great pain, a great depression or a great hope in one's life … otherwise one would not consider such a great undertaking.

But maybe one is just curious – which is quite a solid motivation. Or one has an intuition from which one sets out on the path to one's own center.

I 1. a) Be present

Just sit down and be completely present – at home in an armchair, on the bank of a river or on a bench under an old oak tree.

How do you feel? What are you looking forward to? What are you afraid of? Who are you? How is your body? How about relationships? What about your health? What about your job? What about your money?

Ask yourself some questions and see what the answers are. And then let the questionsgo and just look – into yourself, into the world in front of you … and feel what is there …

I 2. Fire: Wanting to Change Life

Feeling pain or sensing joy is not enough to make a decision. One must also face these feelings, "These are my feelings."

If one pushes these feelings aside and represses them, nothing happens – then one does not set out on the path to oneself.

I 2. a) Look, feel, embrace.

While sitting there, start again to look at what is going on in your life right now and to feel what is going on right now. Then look at what the most important, pressing feeling is.

Imagine yourself standing in front of you with this feeling – how old is this "feeling ego"? As old as yourself? In puberty? A small child?

Take this "feeling self" lovingly in your arms – just like a small child who cries because it has hurt itself.

I 2. b) "It's my life!"

Say to yourself whenever something special happens, or just when you're thinking about it, "It's my life."

This very simple meditation makes you awake, it makes you present, it helps to get out of the daily grind, to leave the vegetative stupor, to really be there …

Then, after a while, one will probably want to live properly.

I 3. Air: The Search for a Way

No one moves unless he sees a way. Perceiving the pain and deciding to look at it is not enough. One needs an idea of how to change the situation.

This is where the mind is called upon: What are the possibilities? And which possibilities look promising?

I 3. a) Information

Ask friends, read books, attend seminars or therapy – and above all, take time to think for yourself about the situation that is bothering you.

Do you know it all too well? What have you already tried? What would be a completely different behavior in this situation?

Wish for an omen, a hint, a good advice.

I 4. Water: The Confidence in the Possibility

Now there is already the pain, the contemplation of the pain and a possible way. Now the trust is needed that one can really go this way, that this way is really possible for oneself.

Here you need trust in yourself – and trust in the world. This trust in the world can be directed to a deity, to life itself, to providence and to some other things.

One needs a support.

I 4. a) Prayer

Sit quietly and turn to your soul, to Christ, to Buddha, to Isis, to Life – to whomever. Ask for help and keep your heart, eyes and hands open.

I 5.   Earth: The First Step

Every path begins with the first step. This first step or this next next step is always the most important of all steps – you have to take it.

When you have seen your feelings, looked at them as your own, searched for a way and also found trust, you must now also go – otherwise nothing will happen.

I 5. a)   The resolution ritual

It helps to make a decision formally. It doesn't have to be a big ceremony, but you should see which form is most suitable.

What do I want? What time feels good? What place fits well? Do I want to wear certain clothing? Do I want to have certain statues, symbols or the like with me?

The most important thing is a witness. If you perform a ritual alone, there is a danger that it will "stay inside". If you have a witness with you, the ritual and also the decision is "outside" – the decision is grounded by the witness.

The ritual itself is very simple:

- Invite one or more deities, if you want them present.

- Invite their soul, your center – it is what you are looking for (otherwise you probably wouldn't be reading this book).

- Say what you want. Formulate your resolution in a way that is right for you – that is the only important thing.

There are also traditional formulas for this resolution to find one's own soul, one's own center, the Higher Self or whatever you want to call this center, but a resolution formulated by yourself is more alive.

I 5. b)   The inner step

In many cases it is useful to keep the resolution alive, i.e. to make oneself aware from time ro time of what one wants and why one wants it. For this, it is often enough to pause for a moment in the morning, during which one feels oneself and also what one wants, as well as what one hopes for from today – this is a short reflection on oneself.

Of course, one can also change one's own direction from time to time on the basis of experiences or realizations, and for this one can also modify one's own resolution in such a way that it is "right" again.

I 5. c) The outer step

The essential point is the outer step: What does one do concretely in the world to get where one wants to go? You don't have to know the whole way, but you have to take a step and then see what the next meaningful step could be.

II First Contact

Finding one's center begins with a first contact – whatever that contact may be.

II 1. Light: Finding Identity

You can sit down and ask your own soul to show itself – as an inner image, as an inner voice, as a sign outside, as an inspiration – whatever. You can also ask it to guide you – this should be done in a way that feels good.

You can also start an inner conversation with your soul and see what comes as a response. The goal of this conversation, by its very nature, is to recognize your own identity.

II 1. a) Conversation aids

If you wish, you can also use a pendulum, automatic writing, tarot cards, etc. as aids to enter into a conversation with your soul.

However, there are two points to keep in mind: First, you should strive to gradually get along without these aids and perceive your soul directly, and second, you should be cautious about everything you perceive in this way and check what you have heard or seen inwardly before you believe or implement it.

The soul is the scriptwriter and you yourself are the director – the soul is the entrepreneur and you yourself are the manager … but you still have the responsibility for the shaping of your own life – and you should not give this responsibility out of your hand.

The inner voice of the soul is very enriching, but you should always be aware that you don't know who it is that has spoken in you: your own soul or a fear, an addiction, an old trauma …

You should not leave your judgment at the checkroom when you sit down to meditate.

II 2. Fire: Finding Strength

To walk a path, one needs determination, courage and strength – three fire qualities.

II 2. a) Request to Michael

One can turn to the Archangel of Fire, Michael, in order to obtain these three qualities or to promote them in oneself. One can also turn directly to the fire, if this is more congenial to one. If you are at home in a certain mythology, you can also turn to one of the fire deities from that mythology: to the North Germanic fire god Loge, to the Egyptian lion goddess Sachmet, to the Indian ecstasy and meditation god Shiva, etc.

Approach Michael (or the deity you have chosen) inwardly and ask for what you wish from him. Listen and see what you get in response. Feel free to ask further – a conversation may arise from it …

And look the fire archangel Michael in the eyes during the conversation.

II 2. b) Self-protection

Can you protect your surrounding space? This is an important point in life … You can play a game in pairs:

> 1. experiment: Person A stands there with his eyes closed. Person B walks slowly and quietly towards A. A says "now" when he feels that B is entering his space.
> The same is repeated while A stands with his back to B, then with his right side to the approaching B, and then with his left side.

> 2. experiment: A stands with his eyes open. B walks slowly towards A. A says "Stop!" or similar when B gets too close to him. If the "Stop!" sounds convincing, B stops – if it doesn't sound convincing, B just keeps walking …

To gain more steadiness, A can imagine a tiger in front of him, an oak tree behind him, ask a deity for help, etc.

The goal is to gain a sense of one's own space and how to protect it in normal everyday life.

II 3.   Air: Finding Clarity

To be able to walk one's own path, clarity is also extremely useful – this is an air quality. Instead of "clarity" you can also say "truth", "realization", "rightness" or something similar, if that suits you more.

II 3. a)   Request to Raphael

Sit down and inwardly ask the Air Archangel Raphael for clarity, truth, realization, etc. Start a conversation with him. See what he looks like. Is there a scent emanating from him? Do you hear a sound? Against what background do you see him?

Of course it is helpful if you already have some practice with meditations, dream journeys, family constellations, automatic writing, pendulums or something similar.

Ask him for the things, you would like to receive from him.

And look Raphael in the eyes!

II 3. b)   The horoscope

Calculate your own horoscope and draw it. Interpret it for yourself or have it interpreted for you. Try to understand the basic principles of a horoscope.

The birth horoscope of a person describes his lifestyle. It is not the soul itself, but at least the garment one's soul has put on in its present incarnation.

A horoscope consists of several elements, which you should be able to distinguish if you want to understand your own horoscope:

- The Ascendant is the stage set, that is, the way one sees the world and how one moves in it.

- The planets are the actors in one's life drama: the Moon is the child, Mercury the student, Venus the youth, Sun the king, Mars the warrior, Jupiter the manager, Saturn the preserver, Uranus the inventor, Neptune the artist, and Pluto the magician.

- Each of these actors is given a role – that is, the sign of the zodiac in which they stand: spontaneous Aries, enjoying Taurus, curious Gemini,

14

sensitive Cancer, self-centered Leo, meticulous Virgo, aesthetic Libra, provocative Scorpio, idealistic Sagittarius, steady Capricorn, cosmopolitan Aquarius, and dreamy Pisces.

- Each actor is also given a place on stage – these are the astrological houses: 1. here and now, 2. kitchen, 3. meeting place, 4. bedroom, 5. king's hall, 6. workshop, 7. living room, 8. battlefield, 9. lookout tower, 10. office, 11. clubhouse, and 12. village square.

- The play itself is determined by the relationships between the actors – these are the astrological aspects: the conjunction is like a marriage, the trine is like a friendship, the sextile is like an acquaintance, the opposition is a swinging complementary opposition, the square is a widening tentpole, the quincunx is an endless again and again ordering, the semi-sextile is the urge to evolve, and then there are planets without aspects performing a solo.

- Furthermore there is the director of the play – this is the ego, which has to make sure that the play gets a good level.

- And if the director gets stuck, he can turn to the scriptwriter this is the own soul (this case is what this book is about).

You can understand your own horoscope better and better throughout your life – and also the horoscopes and lifestyles of other people. It is good to have at least a solid foundation in astrology, because then you understand your own style better – and because you then understand how very different other people are …

This second insight helps to stop trying to imitate others or to convert others to one's own views. Both is extremely helpful if one wants to find oneself.

II 3. c) The chakras

The seven main chakras are created by the radiation of the soul: The heart chakra is the "temple of the soul", the three chakras below it radiate into the body and the three chakras above it radiate into the world.

In the heart chakra lies the identity – it is one's own center, the deep sleep consciousness, one's own inner sun.

Below this "sun chakra" are the "rays" of the solar plexus: the physical self-expression, the impulses directed into the body, the subconsciousness, the physical feelings.

Above this "sun chakra" are the "rays" of the throat chakra: the social self-expression, the impulses directed into the world, the subconsciousness, the social feelings.

Below the solar plexus are the forms of the hara: the inner hold, the inner forms, the waking consciousness, the point of view, the thoughts.

Above the throat chakra are the forms of the third eye: the outer hold, the outer forms, the waking consciousness, the orientation, the thoughts.

Below the hara is the experience of the root chakra: the physical contact, the physical and sexual ecstasy.

Above the third eye is the experience of the crown chakra: the mental contact, the mental and meditative ecstasy.

It is useful to pay attention to whether one overemphasizes one of these chakras – whether one feels pain there, whether the body becomes particularly fat there, whether one feels pressure there, whether one tries to solve almost all situations with the help of the qualities of only one of these seven chakras.

Distinctive one-sidedness can occur:

- with feelings of <u>deficiency</u>:
    - life force congestion in the root chakra and life force deficiency in the crown chakra: <u>addictive</u>
    - life force congestion in the crown chakra and life force deficiency in the root chakra: <u>ascetic</u>

- in power <u>conflicts</u>:
    - life force congestion in the hara and life force deficiency in the third eye: <u>perpetrator</u>
    - life force congestion in the third eye and life force deficiency in the hara: <u>victim</u>

- in case of <u>self-esteem problems</u>:
    - life force congestion in the solar plexus and life force deficiency in the throat chakra: <u>star</u>
    - life force congestion in the throat chakra and life force deficiency in the solar plexus: <u>fan</u>

The ideal state is the balance of life force in the three pairs of chakras, that is, in the six outer chakras, because then the identity in the heart chakra radiates outward in self-love. Then it becomes self-expression in the solar plexus and throat chakra, afterwards power in the hara and third eye, and finally the experience of fullness in the root chakra and crown chakra.

II 3. d) The next step

Have you ever participated in a family constellation? Then there is a practical tool that you can use at any time and for many things: Since in every path you want to take, the next step is the essential thing, you can see it more clearly with the help of a little constellation.

This constellation consists of five positions on which you stand one after the other and see what you feel, see and hear there. These five positions are arranged like the dots on the dice at the "5".

"Next Step" Constellation		
	5. goal	
3. obstacle	2. next step	4. help
	1. starting point	

You stand on the starting point and see how the current situation feels.

Go to the goal and see how it feels.

Return to the starting point and go from there to the center and feel the next helpful step.

When you have identified it, go to point 3 and see what has prevented you from taking the upcoming next step so far.

At point 4, one finds the help that enables oneself to dissolve the obstacle and take the next step.

Finally, one returns once again to point 5, to the goal. One absorbs this quality before dissolving the constellation again.

II 4. Water: Finding Love

To be able to go one's own way, love is also very beneficial: love for oneself, love for others, love from others … one does not have to go one's way alone.

II 4. a) Request to Gabriel

Sit down and speak inwardly to the water archangel Gabriel. Listen … look … feel … What do you perceive? Maybe a feeling? Or an impulse?

First of all, just accept everything that comes and look at it. Answer it or ask a new question or ask for something, for love in your life …

Examining the answers and judging them and deciding what to do next comes only after the meditation, after the dream journey. Judging and critizising during the dream only disturbs the perception.

And look Gabriel in the eyes – otherwise you will miss the best.

II 4. b) Dream journey to one's own center

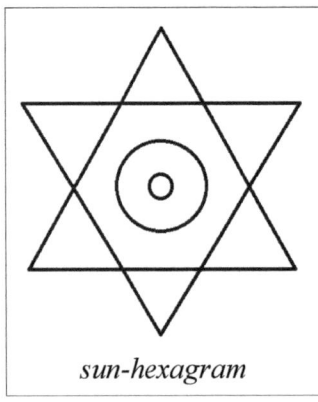

sun-hexagram

In the dream journey to one's own center, you can use different symbols as a door through which you pass at the beginning of the dream journey to define where the dream journey leads. In my experience, the hexagram with the sun in the center leads to the most elaborate visions.

Other possible symbols for the dream journey to one's own center are, for example, the Indo-Germanic sun symbol (circle with a cross in it: ⊗) and the Chinese kien symbol ("heaven" in the I Ching: ☰).

On this dream journey, one wanders to the center of the landscape or the like into which one has entered through the gate with the hexagram.

You can recognize the center by the fact that it is in the middle: a crossroads, a temple, a mountain, an island, a lake, and so on. There you will find a figure, a light, a sun, a sphere, a golden chalice, a precious stone or similar. This is the shape the soul has taken to make its quality understandable to the dream traveler. More precisely this quality is the character of the current incarnation of your soul, i.e. you.

Go to this place again and again and talk to your soul there – preferably daily for a longer period of time. Ask her if she wants to tell or show you something.

And ask her if you may enter into her with your consciousness. Take your time to feel how this feels.

It is very helpful, but not absolutely necessary, to do this dream journey with someone who has already found their soul.

II 5.   Earth: Finding Thriving

Ultimately, all that is needed to find one's way to oneself results in thriving, in well-being, in joy, in growth, in self-experience.

II 5. a)   Request to Auriel

Sit down, gather yourself inwardly and speak to the Earth Archangel Auriel. Ask him something, let him show you something, ask him to prosper.
And – as I said – look Auriel in the eyes.

II 5. b)   The Lesser Pentagram Ritual

The Lesser Pentagram Ritual is a protection ritual and a ritual for obtaining life force. It is structured as follows:

- Kabbalistic cross: centering
- Circle: protection
- Pentagrams: protection, invocation of the elements
- Archangel invocation: invocation of the elements
- Kabbalistic cross: centering

The ritual:

1. Kabbalistic cross: *"Ateh Malkuth ve-Geburah ve-Gedulah le-Olam Amen."*

2. With the index and middle fingers of the right hand, indicate the drawing of the circle on the ground, imagining the circle – repeat twice; imagine the circle clearer each time.

3. Draw with your right hand (gesture and imagination) the eastern pentagram (an up-right pentagram pointing upwards with one point and downwards with two points; one starts from bottom left to top center, further to bottom right, to left center, horizontally to right center, to bottom left).

20

Hold your hand in the center of the imagined pentagram and chant, *"Yod-He-Vau-He"* (Element Air).

4. In the same way, draw the southern pentagram and chant *"Adonai"* (Element Fire).

5. In the same way, draw the western pentagram and chant *"Eheieh"* (element of water).

6. In the same way, draw the northern pentagram and chant *"Agla"* (element earth).

7. Stand in the cross posture (arms outstretched to both sides) facing east and say and imagine:

> *"In front of me Raphael,*
>> (yellow-violet archangel of the air, holding a sword, in the background clouds),
> *behind me Gabriel,*
>> (blue-orange archangel of water, holding a chalice, in the background the sea),
> *to my right hand Michael,*
>> (red-green archangel of fire, holding a staff, flames in the background),
> *to my left hand Auriel;*
>> (lemonyellow-olive-redbrown-black archangel of the earth, holding a coin, in the background fields, pastures and forests),
> *I stand in the middle of the circle,*
>> (strengthen the imagination of the circle)
> *around me are flaming hexagrams,*
>> (the four elements)
> *and above me shines the six-pointed star."*
>> (Hexagram = symbol of the seven planets with the sun in the center).

8. Kabbalistic Cross: *"Ateh Malkuth ve-Geburah ve-Gedulah le-Olam Amen."*

The Kabbalistic cross is performed as follows:

The Kabbalistic Cross		
Words (Aramaic)	**Translation**	**Gesture**
Ateh	Yours is	the left hand comes down from above and touches the forehead with the fingertips
Malkuth	the kingdom	the hand continues down the line that began above the head until the hand points to a point below the feet, marking the vertical bar
ve-Geburah	and the power	the fingertips touch the right shoulder
ve-Gedulah	and the glory	the fingertips go over to the left shoulder and touch it, thereby drawing the crossbeam of the cross
le-Olam, Amen.	in eternity, amen.	both hands are folded in front of the chest, symbolically connecting both beams, imagining a red rose at the point of intersection

The pentagrams (★) symbolize the four elements and the quintessence (upper tip).

The hexagram (✡) represents the seven classical planets: on the outside the Moon, Mercury, Venus, Mars, Jupiter and Saturn, and in the middle the Sun. As in the dream journey to one's own center, the hexagram is also a symbol of one's own center in the pentagram ritual: In the four directions stand the four archangels, with whose help you can express and live your own soul, which is symbolized above you by the hexagram, in your life – and then enjoy that …

It is best to perform the pentagram ritual daily for a few months – and take your time to talk to the archangels and feel the hexagram above you. Be attentive to the effect this simple ritual has on you.

It can have a great effect: The four elements in the four directions evoke the center of the mandala – and that is the quintessence, the soul in your heart chakra … it is the center of this element mandala, this ritual.

II 5. c)   The Middle Pillar Exercise

This ritual connects with God and invokes a blessing from Him. It can be used in many ways as a part of more complex rituals – for example, as centering, strengthening, protection, and also as establishing the connection with one's own soul.

The middle, golden one of the five spheres imagined in this exercise represents one's own soul in one's heart chakra.

A few handbreadths above the head, Kether is imagined as a glistening white sphere and the name of God of Kether is intoned, i.e. sung on a constant tone as full-sounding as possible and ideally with overtones and the natural vibrato of the voice: *"Eheieh"*.

"Kether" and the still following four Hebrew names of the Sephiroth designate the five areas on the Middle Pillar of the Kabbalistic Tree of Life. The names that are chanted are four of the ten traditional names of God of the Old Testament – all these names designate one of the Sephiroth (spheres) on the Tree of Life. However, these names from the original Hebrew of the Old Testament are often not literally translated into German in the Bible, but are simply translated as "God" or "Yahweh."

This chanting of a name of God has similarities with Gregorian chanting and with the Indian and Tibetan way of chanting mantras. This kind of intonation of "holy words" is found among almost all peoples – for example, the ancient Egyptian magicians praised their texts in the papyri as "spells that can be sung well" and in the Germanic myths and sagas it is mentioned again and again that things are consecrated, i.e. charged with magical power, by singing into them ("He sang runes into the sword."; "He sang runes into the forepart of the dragon boat."). However, it is quite sufficient for the beginning to simply chant the names of the gods as sonorously as possible.

On the crown of the head, that is, at the seat of the crown chakra, Da'ath is imagined as a sphere shining in the colors of the rainbow, and Da'ath's name of God is intoned: *"Yod-He-Vau-He Elohim"*.

In the center of the chest, that is, at the seat of the heart chakra, Tiphareth is imagined as a sphere shining golden yellow, and the God-name of Tiphareth is intoned: *"Yod-He-VauHe Eloha va-Daath"*.

4. Around the genitals, i.e. at the seat of the root chakra and thus of the kundalini serpernt, Yesod is imagined as a violet glowing sphere and the god-name Yesod is intoned: *"Shaddai el-Chai"*.

5. Under the feet, i.e. in the earth, Malkuth is imaginated as a brown sphere and the God-name of Malkuth is intoned: *"Adonai ha-Aretz"*.

In the following table the areas, the Sephiroth, the colors, the places and the names of God are summarized again:

The Middle Pillar						
Area	*Sephirah*	*Trans-lation*	*Color*	*Place*	*Name of God*	*Translation*
Unity (God)	Kether	crown	white	sky	*Eheieh*	*I am I*
boundless realm	Da'ath	know-ledge	rainbow colors	crown chakra	*Yod-He-Vau-He Elohim*	*god of wind/ souls – deity*
delimited area	Tiphareth	beauty	golden	heart chakra	*Yod-He-Vau-He Eloha va-Daath*	*god of wind/ souls – deity of knowledge*
internal area	Yesod	foun-dation	violet	root chakra	*Schaddai el-Chai*	*mighty mountain*
multiplicity (world)	Malkuth	king-dom	brown	earth	*Adonai ha-Aretz*	*lord of the earth*

II 5. d) Relaxation

A very simple method of getting closer to oneself is relaxation – both physical and psychological relaxation.

Allowing what is there … seeing what is there … feeling what is there … embracing what is there ….

With this attitude no passivity is meant and also no "letting everything happen", but an arrival, a "being there, where one is". One perceives how it is right now.

In the psyche and in the body there are often several conflicting impulses at the same time, which lead to tension. By conscious relaxation, one perceives these cramps and can look at them and relax them – thus becoming much more effective in what one subsequently does.

Relaxation is not laziness, but healing – one comes closer to oneself again … one relaxes from the periphery to the center, one returns from the outer edge back to the middle.

III Becoming Familiar

The first contact with one's own center is followed by becoming familiar with it: One approaches one's own center in various further ways and can thereby grasp the meaning of one's own soul more and more clearly. One strengthens the contact to one's own soul, whereby it begins to shine more and more in one's own life.

III 1. Light: Here and Now

The Mahasiddha Maitripa formulated a beautiful meditation instruction about 1000 years ago: "to relax into the here and now".

This sounds very simple, but it contains great wisdom. Life is only here and only now – even if perception and thinking can extend to the past and the future.

III 1. a) Being awake

Being truly awake is not as easy as it may sound at first. When one is really awake, one perceives one's whole surroundings and also one's whole inner being. You feel and see and hear and taste and touch …

Try to eat a strawberry and act as if you had never eaten a strawberry before. Listen once to a blackbird and listen as if you had never heard a blackbird before. Look at the sunset glow and look as if you had never seen a sunset glow before.

You can also eat the strawberry as if it were your last strawberry, listen to the blackbird as if it were the last time, give a kiss to a loved one as if that were your last kiss …

III 2.   Fire: One's Own Actions

What is your relationship with fire? When was the last time you sat by an open fire? What would be the most courageous act for you? When was the last time you really enjoyed sex? What do you really want to do – here and now? Is it what you are doing right now? Or would that be something else?

III 2. a)   Dissolving obstacles

What is bothering you in your life? Consider yourself as the cause of it. How would you have to be that you can no longer be disturbed by it?

Who or what is disturbing you? Is it an extreme? (e.g. addiction) What does the counter-extrem look like? (e.g. asceticism) What is the relationship between the two extremes? Do you find this counter-extreme also in yourself?

Take one pole imaginatively in one hand and the other pole in the other hand. Are they both fighting against each other?

What does one pole want? Imagine that what this pole wants rests in the elbow of this one of you arms. Do the same with other pole.

What did one pole originally want in former times – in the very beginning? Imagine this original wish near your heart chakra. Do the same with other pole.

Did both motivations originally have their root in your heart chakra? What was the original impulse – before the split into two poles?

Look at this impulse, feel it, embrace it … stay with it and let it shine in you again.

III 2. b)   The sun

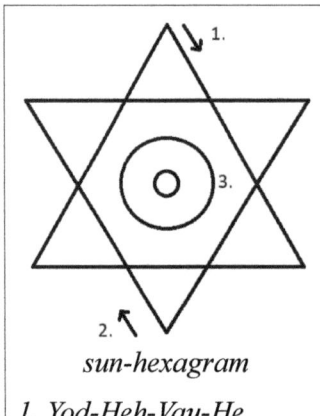

sun-hexagram

1. *Yod-Heh-Vau-He*
2. *Eloah va-Da'Ath*
3. *Ararita*

There is a simple sun ritual that helps to strengthen one's center. Actually, it does not help to strengthen the center, but to give space again to one's own center in one's own psyche and in one's own life.

You can draw this hexagram in the air in front of you: first the upright triangle (1), then the other triangle (2) and finally the sun in the middle (3).

While doing this, one chants/intones the three words indicated under the hexagram – the first two names of God are the same as in the middle, golden heart chakra sphere in the Middle Pillar exercise.

This hexagram can be drawn one after the other in the east, south, west, north, top, bottom and finally three times in the centre. In this way, one creates a "sun-space", a temple of the center.

You may also start with the Lesser Pentagram Ritual. After this the "sun-space" can be built up in the center of the circle of the Pentagram Ritual, under the upper hexagram of the Pentagram Ritual, thus all around oneself – a "sun-temple" …

III 2. c)   The Kundalini

Awakening the Kundalini is for most people a more extensive undertaking, requiring much time, perseverance and commitment. It is one of the most thorough methods of dissolving all inner blockages. When the life force begins to flow again as Kundalini, it pushes against everything within oneself that does not correspond to who one really is. By this, these distortions of one's character become conscious and one can heal them.

The initial meditation is simple:

- One sits down and breathes.

- While inhaling one speaks "fire" inwardly. Inhaling, one takes in life force with the breath, imagining it as light or fire, and directs it to the root chakra.

- While exhaling one speaks "fire" inwardly. Exhaling, ine lets this life force glow in the root chakra.

- All the time you imagine a red-hot sphere in the root chakra, which becomes hotter and hotter.

This is of course only the start of the awakening of the Kundalini. With most people the awakening of the Kundalini is a longer journey, but it might also happen in a rather short time. (If you like, you may find more information in may book "Kundalini for beginners".)

III 2. d) The two companions of the soul

When one approaches one's own soul, it may happen that in a dream, in half-sleep, on a dream journey or during meditation, one sees two figures that seem like siblings. They usually appear only in crises to help one. They are the two companions of the soul who seem to be its "siblings".

If the soul has the form of a man, these siblings have the form of two women. If the soul has the form of a woman, these siblings have the form of two men.

They can be trusted.

III 2. e) The three allies

The life force body of a fertilized egg is shaped by four things:

1. by the DNA of the parents (it becomes a human being),

2. by the dynamics of expansion (a chakra system is formed),

3. by the horoscope (which becomes visible at birth, but is determined beforehand and shapes also the development until birth), and

4. by the character and intentions of the soul for its present incarnation.

Since in the field of the life force similar things are connected with each other, there arise three connections:

1. The dynamics of the soul and its intention cause a connection to an animal: the power animal of the person concerned. This is the animal whose dynamics resemble most closely the dynamics of the soul and its intentions.

2. The posture of the soul and its intention cause a connection to a plant: the power plant of the person concerned. This is the plant whose posture resemble most closely the posture of the soul and its intentions.

3. The structure of the soul and its intention cause a connection to a mineral: the power stone of the person concerned. This is the stone whose structure resemble most closely the structure of the soul and its intentions.

These three are often found "incidentally" when one makes a dream journey to one's own center, i.e. to one's own soul. However, one can also undertake a dream journey with the purpose of finding these three companions.

They are a great help, because by them one can understand how one acts (power animal), stands in the world (power plant) and how one structures oneself and the world (power stone).

III 3.   Air: One's Own thinking

Can you grasp your situation clearly? Can you describe it in striking words? Are you able to understand other people's points of view? Are you able to recognize your own errors and change your mind?

III 3. a)   The center of the horoscope

A simple experiment: Place your horoscope on the floor with the ascendant pointing to the east. Draw the ten planetary symbols on ten sheets of paper and place these sheets in a circle at a distance of one to two meters around the horoscope – in such a way that all planets lie in the same direction on this circle as they do in the horoscope. The paper-plant circle is now your horoscope in large, but without the aspects. Now take away the horoscope form.

Step into the center of the circle – you are the director of this horoscope.

It sounds simple, but the experience is worth it.

III 3. b)   The seven steps of life

Look at the seven steps of life. Where do you stand in terms of your age? Where do you stand from your development? At what age did you have a "shipwreck"? Talk with yourself – that is, with the figure you had at that age (e.g., with seven-year-old John or with fourteen-year-old Susan). This is a kind of dream journey – an inner conversation.

These seven steps of developement are identical in biography and history. Most "shipwrecks" happen in the first three phases of the biography of a man.

These seven steps are:

1. oral phase and Paleolithic: Both are characterized by a symbiosis with the environment: a "yes".

2. anal phase and Neolithic: Both are characterized by the importance of demarcation and shaping the environment while maintaining insertion into the rhythm of the environment: a "No!"

3. phallic phase and kingship: Both are a central control of the whole, the

31

subordination of the system to a center, the shaping of the whole by a single will: an "I!!!"

4. genital phase and materialism: Both are a researching and using, a getting to know and enjoying, an exploring and shaping, an encountering and examining and choosing: a "You?"

5. Adult phase and globalization: Both create a solid connection, a stable system, a sustainable foundation: a "We".

6. tutorial phase and future I: Both expand the possibility, seek new variations, new encounters, learn and teach, give and receive: an "Other …"

7. gerontal phase and future II: Both seeks unity, essence, wisdom, freedom: the "all".

This conversation of the today-self with the younger past-self helps to heal the "shipwreck" in some former pont in one's own biography. Usually these „shipwrecked parts" are more or less isolated in one's own psyche. The conversation with these parts helps to re-integrate them.

There are five points that should be heeded in these conversations:

1. Stay with your feet firmly on the earth. Don't let your head sink unter water. Otherwise you will not be able to integrate anything. If the experience gets to intense, say good bye and leave the conversation. Continue this meeting with your younger self at another time.

2. First just ask and listen and look. Try to understand the situation of your younger self.

3. Try to feel the emotions of your younger self. See what happens inside your younger self.

4. Embrace your younger self. Bid him or her welcome back home.

5. If there are other persons, who have been important at the time of the "shipwreck", invite also the persons to your meetings.

6. Don't hasten – take your time. This is not buidling, this is growing. This ist not welding and not cooking – this is breeding

III 3. c)   The biography

Take a closer look at your own biography. Write down the most important events. Talk about them with someone you know. Look for patterns and repetitions – but above all for crises, transformations and healings, because by them you can learn how to grow.

III 3. d)   The family tradition

Take a very large sheet of paper – the back of a piece of wallpaper or similar. Write down your own name, the names of your relationship partners, siblings, parents, children, grandchildren, grandparents, uncles, aunts, friends, etc. – all those of whom you know something. Write them down as a kind of expanded family tree.

Now write down the zodiac sign, occupation, illnesses, divorces, temperament, age at death, etc. of these people. See if things repeat, if there are similar destinies, relationship patterns, dynamics, etc.

In this way it gradually becomes clear which family tradition you yourself are influenced by – in most cases without being aware of it …

III 4.   Water: One's Own Feelings

How do you feel? How well do you know your inner images? How do you deal with your dreams? Do you have a relationship?

III 4. a)   The dream diary

Writing down your dreams in the morning is the easiest way to get to know your inner imagery better.

First of all, you may see and feel which images are important in you right now, i.e. "charged with life force" or "emotionally charged".

You can simply count which motifs appear how often – this enables a first overview.

Secondly, one can look at which images appear together several times – there must be a connection between them.

Thirdly, one may have a closer look at a particularly striking motif (sex, murder, blood, happiness, etc.). With which other motifs this striking motif appears together in the dreams – in this way one can recognize the "associative environment" of this motif.

Fourth, you may look at what a striking motif reminds you of, i.e. what associations you have with it. Then may you look at which association you have to this association and so on – by these chains of associations you can find hidden motifs.

Fifth, you may get an overall picture: Which dreams belong together? Which motifs belong together? How have some motifs evolved? In this way one can find more and more complex structures, out of which finally the "inner mythology" emerges.

Sixth, one can make dream journeys to the prominent motifs and explore them in more detail.

Seventhly, one may return from the waking state to important dreams and change and reshape them – not in the sense of a lie and a repression, but for example by saving oneself from a dream emergency situation or by giving oneself in the dream what one desperately needed and searched for in the dream.

Thus, one consciously develops the dream into a more peaceful state – one shows the subconscious mind possible solutions, which the subconscious mind then integrates into its image treasure, which is the basis for one's own behavior in everyday life.

By this method of "after dream imagining" one adds new images to the inner mythology, i.e. to the whole of the inner images that may be seen in dreams and in dream journeys.

Eighth, if it fits your situation, you can use a method of some Amerindian tribes: If the dream is possibly important for others as well, one tells the dream in front of the others, performing it like a little play.

But, as I said, for this the situation and the group must fit.

III 4. b)   The dream journey to one's own center

The following "semi-guided dream journey" or "dynamic imagination" originates from the Golden Dawn tradition. The temple in this dream journey is again the heart chakra.

You are walking through a desert. Gradually the scenery becomes clearer and you can see further. You walk on a road that leads to the gate of a city in the desert. The guard lets you in.

You walk through the city to your center. There are avenue trees along the streets and streams and small rivers flowing along their edges. Gradually you will see people in the city. After a while you are also noticed and greeted by them and you greet them back.

You come to the temple in the middle of the city. It is round and has a golden domed roof that is open at the top center. Go to the center of the temple and ask your soul to come, summon it, yearn for it.

Ignite yourself in prayer.

Do this meditation regularly.

III 4. c)   The journey back

There is another way to reach your own soul: the journey to the past.

> *Relax. Become aware of your present age. Return to the past in steps of 5 years. Each time, look briefly at how you felt at that age.*
>
> *Return to the age of 5 years, to 4 years, 3 years, 2 years, 1 year, 6 months, 3 months, 1 month, 2 weeks, 1 week, 3 days, 2 days, 1 days, shortly after your birth, then your birth itself, then shortly before your birth ...*
>
> *Go back even further – 3 months after your conception, 1 month after conception, 1 week after conception, 1 day after conception, your conception itself ... see what you perceive, what you feel, what impulses you have ...*
>
> *Go back even further to before your conception – look at your conception that is about to happen ... As who or what do you look from before your conception to your future incarnation? How does that feel?*
>
> *Go back even further: how did the decision to incarnate feel? Where did it take place? What impulses came together to form a structure?*
>
> *Go back a step further: what was the impulse for your incarnation? Why did your soul want to incarnate as you? What was your soul's intention when it decided to incarnate?*

You can still go back even further into the realm of deities and search for the "sea of a deity" of which your soul is a "drop" ... but that is no longer part of the search for your own soul.

III 5.   Earth: One's Own Growing

The earth is the thriving, the growing, the well-being, the experiencing, the enjoying … you can also cultivate this …

III 5. a)   Tiphareth

Mark the positions of the eleven Sephiroth of the Kabbalistic Tree of Life on the floor with the help of eleven sheets of paper, on which the names of these Sephiroth are written, so that you now have the Tree of Life in front of you.

> *Now stand consciously as in a family constellation on Malkuth – your body.*
> *Continue to Yesod – your subconscious and life force body.*
> *Go on to Hod – your mind and your inner structures.*
> *Go on to Netzach – your feelings and impulses.*
> *Go on to Tiphareth – your soul with its intention for its present incarnation.*
> *Go on to Geburah – your soul in designing its current incarnation.*
> *Go on to Chesed – your soul with its impulse for its present incarnation.*

You can also go further on to Da'ath, Binah, Chokmah and Kether, but this goes beyond the search for your own soul.

The Tree of Life				
Areas		Sephiroth		
God			Kether: *unity*	
deities		Binah: *protection*		Chokmah: *expansion*
			Da'ath: *mythology*	
soul		Geburah: *karma*		Chesed: *past lives*
			Tiphareth: *incarnation*	
psyche		Hod: *thinking*		Netzach: *feeling*
			Yesod: *dreaming*	
body			Malkuth: *body*	

III 5. b)   The center of the hexagram

Draw a hexagram on the floor or mark the tips and center of the hexagram with seven pieces of paper, each with a planetary symbol:

bottom:	Moon	(= Yesod)
bottom left:	Mercury	(= Hod)
bottom right:	Venus	(= Netzach)
center:	Sun	(= Tiphareth)
upper left:	Mars	(= Geburah)
top right:	Jupiter	(= Chesed)
top:	Saturn	(= Da'ath)

Stand in the middle of the hexagram like in a family constellation. Feel the quality there.

Maybe start by standing in first in the six outer triangles and in the end in the sun-hexagon in the centre of the hexagram.

III 5. c)   The soul constellation

You can also get to know the soul with a normal family constellation.

First of all, you are represented by one person and your soul is represented by another person – they are both placed in the constellation-space. In this part of the constellation you look from the sidelines at what happens.

Later on in the constellation you take over the role of yourself, i.e. you stand as youself in the constellation-space. Now you look from your psyche to your soul – now you are an active part of the constellation.

After this yout take over the role of your own soul, i.e. you stand as your soul in the constellation-space.

Of course, it isn't possible to predict exactly and in detail how such a soul constellation will proceed.

III 5. d) Walking

Walk. Pay attention to how you walk. Limp? Tired? Exhausted? Tense? Stiff? Sagging? Struggling? Stomping? Like a box with legs underneath?
Or joyful, enjoying, elastic, elegant, swinging?

Every movement while walking starts in the feet and swings upwards through the body to the movements of the head – which result from the movements of the feet.
You may have to grope and search for this way of walking for a while. A few questions can help:
Are the muscles of your butt tense? Not hard, but tense in an powerful and elastic way. This is the most important thing while walking.
Are the knees wooden and pushed through or do they swing with a slight, comfortable tension?
Are you in a hollow back?
Is the upper back elastic?
Is the neck neither stiff nor floppy, but flexible?
Do you feel your body as a whole, as a unit, as an organism?

Since every person is different, it is only possible to give concrete tips in personal contact – but everyone can set out in search of the discovery of walking.
It may sound extremely simple, but it is worth it – in the posture while walking you can find yourself in your body – and you may find a lot of feelings, that have been hidden in your hard or floppy muscles …

IV   Deepening

The fourth phase is about deepening what you have already found in the previous phases. This is not only a practice, but also a discovery of new facets and connections … and above all a rejoicing in what one has aalready found and what one may still find in the future.

The search for oneself is above all a search for the joy of life …

IV 1.   Light: Self-Expression

To be what one really is means that one radiates. Identity in the heart chakra becomes uninhibited physical self-expression in the solar plexus and uninhibited social self-expression in the throat chakra. Self-expression becomes the inner hold in the hara and the outer orientation in the third eye. Finally, this becomes the physical contact in the root chakra and the social contact in the crown chakra.

Uninhibited self-expression is radiance … and this radiance brings about magic – the shaping of one's life according to the anticipation of the self-realization which one germinates as a vision within oneself.

IV 1. a)   The invocation of the sun

Stand in a secluded place in the posture of the man-rune facing the sun. This is the invocation posture: one stands erect and raises the arms sideways and upwards into the air. When you apply this rune to the sun, both palms are facing the sun.

Feel the sun on your body and especially on your heart chakra and on your palms.

Chant inwardly or with your voice the runic name "Man". Let it vibrate in your heart chakra and palms by your chanting.

Imagine a connection from the sun to your palms, made of golden light. This light fills you and creates new ways in which your soul can show itself in your life, in which you can express yourself, in which you can radiate, be yourself …

If you are in a crowded area it is nevertheless possible to lean oneself against a wall, let your arms hang down but turn your palms towards the sun and feel your hand chakras "drink" the sunlight – a most simple invocation of the sun. This is an easy help to regain some life force and some inner stability.

IV 1. b)   The sun meditation

Sit down in your preferred meditation posture. Say "sun" inwardly while inhaling and "love" while exhaling. Imagine taking in life force as you inhale and directing it into your heart chakra, where this life force then lights up like a sun as you exhale.

This meditation is simple but effective.

IV 1. c)   The wish list

Write a wish list – what do you wish for?

Now once again, but really unrestrained: To be a billionaire? To be able to fly? To walk on the moon? Have tea with the Dalai Lama? A chat with Socrates? A palace in the Sahara? Travel through space on the Enterprise? Become a Yedi?

Now read these wishes aloud once.

Now once again, but this time as fulfilled wishes – imagine that you have received everything you wished for.

How does that feel? Do you feel the grin, the joy, the happiness, the radiance?

All this is already there in you, as you see …

In you a sun wants to shine and seeks all these wishes just to express itself in them. This sun does not need the fulfillment of desires to be able to shine happily – the sun already shines and needs these desires only to be able to express itself. Happiness is not the goal of actions outside, but the source of actions in one's heart chakra.

The soul brings fullness into the world by its self-expression – it needs nothing from the world to have fullness and happiness within itself.

This "wish game" is a bit more effective if you do it with other people – so they don't know the next step that is coming up.

IV 1. d)   The protective deity

The soul is a "drop" from the "sea of a deity". When you have established contact with your own soul, you can ask your soul to guide you to your own protective deity. Your soul knows how to do this most easily for you. Maybe you find a god or a goddess that has already been of some importance to you.

IV 1. e)   God

If you want, you can travel even further on to God. See what your soul says about this. You can also take a dream journey to Kether or lay out the Tree of Life with labeled pieces of paper and then stand on Kether as you would in a family constellation.

IV 2. Fire: Energy

Life is action, singing, dancing, moving, walking, jumping … "In the beginning was the Deed!" as Goethe so beautifully put it.

IV 2. a) Egoism

Egoism is the urge to keep oneself alive. Without it, one would simply cease to live. Egoism is therefore necessary for life.

However, egoism does not stand alone, but is connected with perceptions, memories, thoughts, with the ability of insight, feelings etc..

A high-class egoism, i.e. an effective egoism, needs several companions as helpers:

Light: The effective egoism is connected, for example, with self-knowledge – otherwise it would strive for things which are not beneficial for the person at all.

Fire: Effective egoism is also connected with courage – otherwise it cannot be realized.

Water: It is also connected with love for oneself and for others – otherwise it could sink into self-doubt and loneliness.

Air: The effective egoism is also connected with foresight – a short-sighted egoism leads to a short-term advantage, but to a medium-term and long-term disadvantage.

Earth: It is also connected with serenity – otherwise it could fall into actionism and panic attacks.

So there is something to be said for taking a closer look at one's own egoism …

IV 2. b)   Tummo, bindhu and sun

There are three main sources of power:

- The first source is the <u>earth fire</u>, which becomes the Kundalini fire in the body. This red, unshaped force is also called "Tummo". It rises from the iron/ nickel core of the earth, which is the root chakra of the earth, into the root chakra of human beings.

One can call this earth fire by sending a ray of light from one's root chakra to the center of the earth and then calling up from there one's own dragon, that is, one's own share of the earth's life force: the Kundalini.

- The second source is the <u>sky light</u>, which flows down from above into the crown chakra. Often it is called by awakening one's own Kundalini and letting it rise up to the crown chakra. However, it is also possible to call down this glistening white light without the awakening of the Kundalini. This is called "milking the sky cow" in the Indian Upanishads.

A simple method for this is the already presented "Exercise of the Middle Pillar".

- The third source is <u>one's own soul</u> in the heart chakra. However, it is a source of power of a different kind – from it new life force does not flow into the person, but it keeps the life force together and directs and concentrates it and directs it towards goals. This source of power is like a golden sun.

For this you can choose one of the many methods of centering in your own heart chakra – for example, meditation with the mantra "Sun – Love".

The earth-fire and the sky-light mix and connect in the chakras and shape their character by creating different mixtures:

- In the crown chakra are 6/6 light: awareness.

- In the third eye are 5/6 light and 1/6 fire: a conscious impulse.

- In the throat chakra are 4/6 light and 2/6 fire: conscious design.

- In the heart chakra are 3/6 light and 3/6 fire: self-love.

- In the solar plexus are 2/6 light and 4/6 fire: directed life force.

- In the hara are 1/6 light and 5/6 fire: centered life force.

- In the root chakra are 6/6 fire: life force.

IV 2. c) Trauma dissolution

A trauma is formed in an existential situation in which one is completely focused on survival: in an accident, in war, in rape, and the like. In this case, the life force activity is "set to maximum" and all available adrenalin is released.

If one survives the situation, the normal reaction is to start shaking, screaming, cursing or laughing in order to release the tension. There may also have been a struggle that caused the tension to dissipate. When the tension is released, everything is okay.

If you are prevented from releasing the tension or if the situation is constantly repeated, the tension remains and becomes chronic. One then has, so to speak, a tin can full of adrenaline and panic images in the cellar of one's psyche, rattling away on the shelf.

Such a "tin can" can hinder the psyche in the long run … and prevent one from living exactly what one really is in all areas.

Now you can't dissolve a trauma with a snap of your fingers and you might need professional help for that.

However, one can generally say that in most cases it makes sense to approach the trauma slowly: one looks at the situations in which one "behaves strangely", one looks at what one knows about it, one approaches it and feels for the emotions in this trauma …

The two important points are that one seeks contact with the feelings in the trauma and at the same time "always keeps one's head above water". If one has no contact to the feelings, one cannot change anything – and if one loses one's head, one cannot create anything.

In very simple terms, trauma healing consists of "looking, feeling, embracing" – although these three things can be a bit more dramatic with trauma than with a normal repressed feeling.

IV 2. d) Fire walking

Sign up for a firewalking seminar. A really hot thing! It is self-explanatory if you take part in it and run barefoot over the glowing coals …

IV 3.   Air: Insights

The deepening also refers to the understanding of oneself, of the structure of one's own psyche, of the intentions of the soul, of the way to oneself, etc. Understanding alone does not help, but without understanding most things are much more difficult to accomplish.

IV 3. a)   Talking with the Archangels

Talk to the archangels, tell them where you are right now, what you want to achieve, what is hindering you, etc. You can do this in the context of the Lesser Pentagram Ritual or without it, only with one archangel or with all four of them one after the other, you can also make a dream journey to them …

Ask for concrete advice – and try out this advice.

IV 3. b)   The planetary round

Place the planetary slips of paper in a circle on the floor in the shape of your horoscope and stand in the centre (as already described in an earlier chapter).

Invite each of the ten planets by addressing them directly.

Ask each planet if it has something to tell you or show you. Take it seriously, ask if you didn't understand something. This is an inner converstion, but sometimes it's helpful to speak your questions aloud.

Start a conversation with your planets, make suggestions on how to solve a conflict between two planets (e.g. if they have a square to each other), listen to what the planets involved have to say …

You can keep your eyes open like in a family constellation or close them like in a dream journey – see what is easiest for you. If you are with a dozen people, you can also do a horoscope family constellation, where each planet is represented by one person and you yourself have the role of the director in the centre.

Once a beginning has been found, the conversation will develop quickly.

IV 3. c)   The inner family

If you have been doing dream journeys, family constellations, "therapeutic self-talk" and the like for a while, you will find your inner child, your inner parents, a version of yourself with the opposite sex, and so on. All these figures, i.e. the "inner family", can be invited once and see what happens when they are all gathered.

The dynamics of this gathering and its benefits are quite similar to the "planetary round".

IV 3. d)   Rightness

There is a quality that is the central element in magical-mythological worldviews: rightness. This quality can be of great help.

It is found in the roundness of the wheel, in the tuning of an instrument, in the straightness of an axis, in the functioning of a machine, in the soundness of the body, in the radiance of the psyche....

This rightness is there when all parts of a whole are in their right place and behave in the right way. If one has the feeling that something is wrong, that there is a disharmony, that a detail simply does not fit with the rest, etc., then it is worthwhile to pursue this discord.

This is also a method to gradually find oneself.

IV 4. Water: Connectedness

Water binds the individual into a community, water can bring love, water gives full-ness, water gives security …

IV 4. a) Feelings and their transformations

Abundance, power from within and self-love are the three basic healing feelings.
When they are disturbed, lack, might and self-doubt arise.
These three painful feelings each become two polar extremes:

abundance	=> lack	=> the "loud" addict and the "quiet" ascetic
power	=> might	=> the "loud" abuser and the "quiet" victim
self-love	=> self-doubt	=> the "loud" star and the "quiet" fan

From these six polarized feelings, a wide variety of feeling nuances emerge. In order to become healed and to be completely oneself, it is necessary to trace this whole variety of feelings back to the three basic healed feelings of abundance, power and self-love.

1. The originals and ideally also the normal state is radiance.

2. If now a ray, i.e. an impulse, encounters an obstacle, astonishment arises, then perhaps displeasure, the search for a way around the obstacle.

3. If this does not succeed, the ray increases its intensity and becomes anger, which wants to clear the obstacle out of the way.

4. If this succeeds, it is good, if not, two different things can happen:

a) Either the rage becomes one-sided, turning into hatred,

b) or it begins to spin in circles, turning into sadness. If this circling begins to become even more slowly and finally stops, it becomes depression.

The way back leads from depression to sadness to anger to strength, and from hatred to anger to strength. These paths are the same for all people.
I have described the great variety of these emotions and their transformations in detail in my book of the same title: "Gefühle und ihre Verwandlungen".

IV 4. b) Reincarnation

If one wants to get to know oneself and therefore one's own soul, one could also get the idea of wanting to know one's own previous incarnations – if one assumes or thinks it possible that reincarnation exists.

For this, one can participate in a past life regression or take a dream journey to Chesed on the Tree of Life, or simply ask one's own soul to show something about one's past lives.

However, this is not absolutely necessary in order to recognize oneself. That which has been taken from a previous life into the present life is "re-enacted" during the first three years, i.e. one experiences things by which one reconnects to the previous undigested experiences – the "karma" is updated in one's life during the first three years.

So it is quite sufficient to heal one's own wounds received by the experiences in one's present life – thus one heals one's karma at the same time.

Nevertheless, it can of course be interesting to see how you got to where you are now in previous lives – but you don't need this knowledge to heal your own past, and you don't need it to be happy.

IV 4. c) The heart meditation

There is a heart meditation in many traditions. What they have in common is that it is focused on the heart chakra. Often it is also an identification with a role model such as Christ, Buddha or Osiris.

The starting point can be quite different: a mantra, the name of the deity, breathing exercises, worship of the deity, Hatha yoga and the like with sun reference, chanting, pilgrimages, bowing, etc.. Often several methods are combined.

If one adds the worship of a deity, this meditation gets a special power – just the help by this deity.

The already described mantra meditation ("Sun – Love") is also a heart meditation.

As with all things, one should see what one is drawn to and then try it out.

IV 4. d)   The silence meditation

Silence meditation is simple to describe (but not necessarily as simple to perform): one becomes inwardly silent.

This means that one stops thinking, feeling, seeing images … one is only consciousness aware of oneself – one has connected one's waking consciousness with one's deep sleep consciousness. Then you are only conscious of your own consciousness – but it's completely quite in there.

The easiest way to reach this state is to meditate together with someone who can already reach this state. Otherwise, one can only practice this state and let go of all contents of consciousness again and again …

But there is a trick, with which you can reach this state for a short time, so that you can get to know its "taste". To do this, you sit down and say out loud what is on your mind. You say faster and faster what the next association, the next image, the next thought is … after quite a short time you then come to a point where simply nothing new appears and you have become completely empty. One has talked oneself empty, so to speak.

It is important that you talk fast and say everything immediately – as if you were running after every new word and every new image, every new feeling. This leads to the fact that the "vessel" is then suddenly empty and it has become quiet in one.

If you have reached the silent state, it stabilizes itself. This feels as if one had climbed a mountain but now one has reached the top and finds there a shallow valley. You may rest there and there is no danger of sliding down the mountain side.

If you dicide to leave this valley again you have use some energy for this – for walking up to the brim of the valley. Afterwards it's quite easy to go down the side of the mountain and thinl, fell and see images again.

IV 5. Earth: Grounding

Ultimately, everything must be grounded – things become real when they appear in the material world. Then they can be lived, experienced and enjoyed.

IV 5. a) The relationship mandala

The relations to other people are beased on an simple inner structure and dynamic, that may maybe found with olmost every man and woman.
This mandala looks like this:

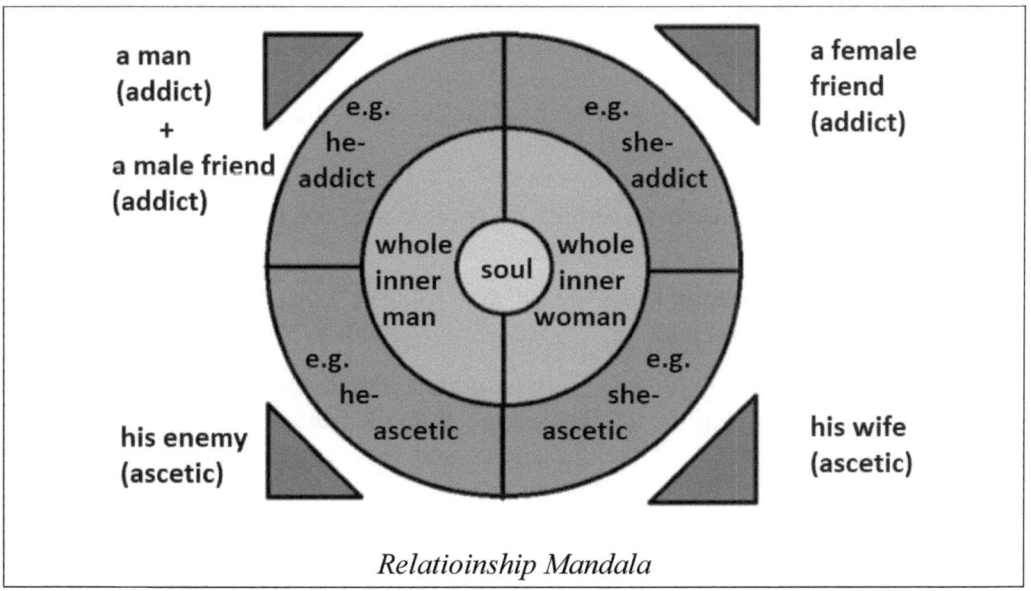

Relatioinship Mandala

The Relationship Mandala has a simple inner structure:

- In the beginning was the soul: the central circle of the mandala.

- The soul is reflected twice in the life force as the inner whole man and as the inner whole woman, which become one's self-image and the search image, respectively: the two semicircles around the central circle.

51

- When polarization occurs in the psyche as a result of a violent experience, it happens either in the realm of abundance (=> addict/ascetic), power (perpetrator/victim) or self-love (=>star/fan). This polarization happens with both the self-image and the "opposite-sex search image". This creates another circular ring consisting of four quarter circles – if the polarization occurred with the abundance theme, which thus becomes a deficiency theme, these four quarter circles represent a he-addict, a he-ascetic, a she-addict and a she-ascetic.

- One of these images is lived by the subject himself (e.g. the he-addict), the other three images are taken by other persons. In the example of the he-addict, the he-ascetic is the enemy, the she-addict is the friend, and the she-ascetic is the relationship partner. Possibly other he-addicts can be friends. These are the four triangles at the edge of the mandala. Together they perform the life drama of the person to which this relationship mandala belongs.

The way of healing of one's own psyche can be derived from the structure of this mandala:

The first step consists simply of recognizing the four roles in one's own drama.

The second step is to accept all four roles as part of one's psyche – that's usually the hardest part.

The third step, if the patient is a he-addict is to dissolve the image of the he-addict and image of the the he-ascetic – then the healed inner man can appear.
Next, the image of the she-addict and the image of the she-ascetic are dissolved – then the wholesome inner woman can appear.

Finally, the wholesome inner man and the wholesome inner woman unite with each other – then the soul can appear.

A detailed description of this mandala and the healing ritual may be found in my book "Das Beziehungs-Mandala".

III 5. b)   The inner man and the inner woman

There is a meditation based on the inner man and the inner woman. This man and this woman correspond to the two outer life force channels that connect the seven main chakras. They are called "Ida" and "Pingala." The main central channel is called "Sushumna" and corresponds to the soul. These three channels correspond to the inner circle and the two semicircles in the relationship mandala.

During meditation, one imagines the inner man and the inner woman in all seven main chakras one after the other. They first sit naked in the lotus position in front of each other on the chakra lotus flower. Then they move towards each other. Finally, the woman sits on the man's lap, wraps her legs around the man's abdomen and unites with him.

It is quite beneficial to feel the erotic tension of this union – you should just hold this tension and enjoy it as long as you want. At some point this tension dissolves into a glow and a radiance – then the life force has arrived at the soul, at the sushumna, at the heart chakra.

IV 5. c)   The initiation rituals of the Golden Dawn

The initiation rituals of the Golden Dawn are complex ceremonies based on the Kabbalistic Tree of Life. If one has an inclination towards ritual magic, these initiation rituals can give a great impetus to live out of one's soul.

These rituals are designed for a group of magicians holding various roles, but one can also perform these rituals alone, constantly changing from one role to another.

IV 5. d)   Walking barefoot

This is a very simple but effective exercise. It has at least two effects: You become more present in the here and now by paying attention to the soles of your feet, and you connect with the earth.

Both also promote self-knowledge and self-expression.

IV 5. e)   Yoga and Sports

Sometimes Hatha yoga, sports, hiking, jogging, swimming, martial arts, etc. are also helpful – especially when one is not really aware of one's own body or sees it almost as something foreign in which sits one's own consciousness.

IV 5. f)   The gardener

In general, the attitude of the gardener is beneficial: being friendly to oneself; taking one's time; "watering" and "weeding"; letting things grow; promoting one's own dynamics; being with what is at the moment, but also not losing sight of the possibilities for development …

V   The radiance

The goal is radiance: unrestrained self-expression, unhindered by any inner contradictions. Every situation is an opportunity to express who you are.

V 1.   Light: The Dance of Life

To dance one's own life, to sing one's own song, to let one's own light shine, to give shape to the qualities of one's own soul in the world by one's own deeds – what else is there to do?

V 2.   Fire: Unfolding

Being constant in action out of one's source, frowing out of one's "heart-seed", but constantly transforming one's own form – to ever greater, more radiating versions.

V 3.   Air: The Song of Life

Write down once what you know about yourself – the name of your soul, your power animal, your ascendant, your preference for a particular musical instrument, your loyalty in friendships, your courage – whatever. Take your time to find as many things as you can that you can wholeheartedly say are true, that describe who you really are.

Put this into simple sentences like "I am …" or "I do …". Line up these sentences so that similar things are next to each other. From this a "Hymn to Myself" can develop.

Read this "Hymn to Myself" aloud – at first best without a listener, later possibly also to a friend.

It is worthwhile.

V 4.   Water: Self-Love

Take time to love yourself – just to feel inside yourself, to feel the radiance in your heart, the source of your egoism … just the self-love that made you come into being. This is something you can feel better than you can describe …

V 5.   Earth: Life

Be true to yourself … live your life … and it will flourish.

English Books by Harry Eilenstein

- Living Magic (261 p.)
- The Synthesis of Physics and Magic (192 p.)
- Telepathy for Beginners (60 p.)
- Telepathy for Advanced Learners (52 p.)
- Telekinesis for Beginners (56 p.)
- Astral Projection for Beginners (60 p.)
- Prophecy for Beginners (60 p.)
- Invocations for Beginners (52 p.)
- Evocations for Beginners (62 p.)
- Auto-Movement for Beginners (60 p.)
- Elves for Beginners (56 p.)
- Hypnosis for Beginners (56 p.)
- Money Magic for Beginners (60 p.)
- Magic Objects for Beginners (64 p.)
- Shamanism for Beginners (52 p.)
- Self Knowledge for Beginners (60 p.)
- Number Symbolism for Beginners (64 p.)
- Crop Circles for Beginners (344 p.)

These books will be puplished soon:
- Life Force for Beginners
- Meditation for Beginners
- Kundalini for Beginners
- Chakra-Magic for Beginners
- Astrology for Beginners
- Ritual Magic for Beginners
- Mandalas for Beginners
- Love Magic for Beginners
- Magic Research for Beginners
- Symbolism of Numbers for Beginners
- Language of the Moon – for Beginners
- Magic Chant for Beginners
- Da'ath-Magic for Beginners
- Feng Shui for Beginners
- Magic for Beginners – Anthology I
- Magic for Beginners – Anthology II
- Magic for Beginners – Anthology III
- Magic for Beginners – Anthology IV

Bücher von Harry Eilenstein

Religion allgemein
- Die sieben Schritte des Lebens (428 S.)
- Muttergöttin und Schamanen (168 S.)
- Göbekli Tepe (472 S.)
- Die Göttin von Göbekli Tepe (144 S.)
- Totempfähle (440 S.)
- Christus (60 S.)
- Dakini (80 S.)
- Vajra (76 S.)

Ägypten
- Hathor und Re 1: Götter und Mythen im Alten Ägypten (432 S.)
- Hathor und Re 2: Die altägyptische Religion – Ursprünge, Kult und Magie (396 S.)
- Isis (508 S.)

Indogermanen
- Die Entwicklung der indogermanischen Religionen (700 S.)
- Wurzeln und Zweige der indogermanischen Religion (224 S.)

Germanen
- Die Götter der Germanen (87 Bände – siehe nächste Seite)
- Odin (300 S.)

Kelten
- Cernunnos (690 S.)
- Taliesin (228 S.)
- Der Kessel von Gundestrup (220 S.)
- Der Chiemsee-Kessel (76)

Psychologie
- Über die Freude (100 S.)
- Das Geheimnis des inneren Friedens (252 S.)
- Das Beziehungsmandala (52 S.)
- Gefühle und ihre Verwandlungen (404 S.)
- einsgerichtet (140 S.)
- Liebe und Eigenständigkeit (216 S.)
- Von innerer Fülle zu äußerem Gedeihen (52 S.)

Heilung
- Die Symbolik der Krankheiten (76 S.)

Kunst
- Herz des Tanzes – Tanz des Herzens (160 S.)

Drama
- König Athelstan (104 S.)

Bücher von Harry Eilenstein

„Magie für Anfänger"

- Telepathie für Anfänger (60 S.)
- Telepathie für Fortgeschrittene (52 S.)
- Telekinese für Anfänger (52 S.)
- Lebenskraft für Anfänger (60 S.)
- Meditation für Anfänger (56 S.)
- Kundalini für Anfänger (100 S.)
- Hypnose für Anfänger (56 S.)
- Auto-Movement für Anfänger (56 S.)
- Chakra-Magie für Anfänger (148 S.)
- Astralreisen für Anfänger (56 S.)
- Astrologie für Anfänger (120 S.)
- Ritual-Magie für Anfänger (56 S.)
- Mandalas für Anfänger (68 S.)
- Geldzauber für Anfänger (56 S.)
- Liebeszauber für Anfänger (52 S.)
- Invokationen für Anfänger (52 S.)
- Evokationen für Anfänger (60 S.)
- Elfen für Anfänger (56 S.)
- Magie-Forschung für Anfänger (140 S.)
- Selbsterkenntnis für Anfänger (52 S.)
- Zahlensymbolik für Anfänger (60 S.)
- Die Sprache des Mondes – für Anfänger (116 S.)
- Zaubergesänge für Anfänger (100 S.)
- Zukunftschau für Anfänger (60 S.)
- Schamanismus für Anfänger (52 S.)
- Magische Gegenstände für Anfänger (68 S.)
- Da'ath-Magie für Anfänger (64 S.)
- Kornkreise für Anfänger (348 S.)
- Feng Shui für Anfänger (96 S.)
- Magie für Anfänger – Sammelband I (696 S.)
- Magie für Anfänger – Sammelband II (664 S.)
- Magie für Anfänger – Sammelband III (580 S.)

„Traumreisen"

- Traumreisen zu Heilpflanzen (700 S.)

Magie

- Handbuch für Zauberlehrlinge (408 S.)
- Tarot (104 S.)
- Physik und Magie (184 S.)
- Die Synthese von Physik und Magie (200S.)
- Die Magie-Formel (156 S.)
- Krafttiere – Tiergöttinnen – Tiertänze (112 S.)
- Schwitzhütten (524 S.)
- Mythen und Magie der Harfe (116 S.)
- Magie heute – Berichte aus der Praxis (288 S.)

Meditation

- Der Lebenskraftkörper (230 S.)
- Die Chakren (100 S.)
- Das Chakren-System mit den Nebenchakren (296 S.)
- Organe und Chakren (64 S.)
- Die platonischen Körper in den Chakren (156 S.)
- Meditation (140 S.)
- Drachenfeuer (124 S.)
- Kundalini I (676 S.)
- Reinkarnation (156 S.)
- einsgerichtet (140 S.)

Astrologie

- Astrologie (496 S.)
- Photo-Astrologie (428 S.)
- Die astrologischen Aspekte (88 S.)
- Horoskop und Seele (120 S.)

Kabbala

- Kursus der praktischen Kabbala (150 S.)
- Eltern der Erde (450 S.)
- Blüten des Lebensbaumes:
    - Die Struktur des kabbalistischen Lebensbaumes (370 S.)
    - Der kabbalistische Lebensbaum als Forschungshilfsmittel (580 S.)
    - Der kabbalistische Lebensbaum als spirituelle Landkarte (520 S.)

Die Themen der 87 Bände der Reihe „Die Götter der Germanen"

1. Die Entwicklung der germanischen Religion
2. Lexikon der germanischen Religion
3. Der ursprüngliche Göttervater Tyr
4. Tyr in der Unterwelt: der Schmied Wieland
5. Tyr in der Unterwelt: der Riesenkönig   Teil 1
6. Tyr in der Unterwelt: der Riesenkönig   Teil 2
7. Tyr in der Unterwelt: der Zwergenkönig
8. Der Himmelswächter Heimdall
9. Der Sommergott Baldur
10. Der Meeresgott: Ägir, Hler und Njörd
11. Der Eibengott Ullr
12. Die Zwillingsgötter Alcis
13. Der neue Göttervater Odin   Teil 1
14. Der neue Göttervater Odin   Teil 2
15. Der Fruchtbarkeitsgott Freyr
16. Der Chaos-Gott Loki
17. Der Donnergott Thor
18. Der Priestergott Hönir
19. Die Göttersöhne
20. Die unbekannteren Götter
21. Die Göttermutter Frigg
22. Die Liebesgöttin: Freya und Menglöd
23. Die Erdgöttinnen
24. Die Korngöttin Sif
25. Die Apfel-Göttin Idun
26. Die Hügelgrab-Jenseitsgöttin Hel
27. Die Meeres-Jenseitsgöttin Ran
28. Die unbekannteren Jenseitsgöttinnen
29. Die unbekannteren Göttinnen
30. Die Nornen
31. Die Walküren
32. Die Zwerge
33. Der Urriese Ymir
34. Die Riesen
35. Die Riesinnen
36. Mythologische Wesen
37. Mythologische Priester und Priesterinnen
38. Sigurd/Siegfried
39. Helden und Göttersöhne
40. Die Symbolik der Vögel und Insekten
41. Die Symbolik der Schlangen, Drachen und Ungeheuer
42.a Die Symbolik der Herdentiere I
42.b Die Symbolik der Herdentiere II
43. Die Symbolik der Raubtiere
44. Die Symbolik der Wassertiere und sonstigen Tiere
45. Die Symbolik der Pflanzen
46. Die Symbolik der Farben
47. Die Symbolik der Zahlen
48. Die Symbolik von Sonne, Mond und Sternen
49.a Das Jenseits I – Das Hügelgrab
49.b Das Jenseits II – Der Jenseitsweg
50. Seelenvogel, Utiseta und Einweihung
51. Wiederzeugung und Wiedergeburt
52. Elemente der Kosmologie
53. Der Weltenbaum
54. Die Symbolik der Himmelsrichtungen und der Jahreszeiten
55.a Mythologische Motive I
55.b Mythologische Motive II
56. Der Tempel
57. Die Einrichtung des Tempels
58. Priesterin – Seherin – Zauberin – Hexe
59. Priester – Seher – Zauberer
60. Rituelle Kleidung und Schmuck
61. Skalden und Skaldinnen
62. Kriegerinnen und Ekstase-Krieger
63. Die Symbolik der Körperteile
64.a Magie und Ritual I
64.b Magie und Ritual II
64.c Magie und Ritual III
65. Gestaltwandlungen
66.a Magische Angriffs-Waffen
66.b Magische Verteidigungs-Waffen
67. Magische Werkzeuge und Gegenstände
68. Zaubersprüche
69. Göttermet
70. Zaubertränke
71. Träume, Omen und Orakel
72. Runen
73. Sozial-religiöse Rituale
74. Weisheiten und Sprichworte
75. Kenningar
76. Rätsel
77. Die vollständige Edda des Snorri Sturluson
78. Frühe Skaldenlieder
79.a Mythologische Sagas I
79.b Mythologische Sagas II
80. Hymnen an die germanischen Götter